Shepherd Leadership

Learning to lead with true power.

By Dr. Steven G. Purdon

*"Do nothing from selfish ambition or conceit,
but in humility count others more significant
than yourselves" -- Philippians 2.3*

Acknowledgments

This book would not have been possible without the contributions from subject-matter experts who provided feedback, opinions, and advice on the content, accuracy, and overall usefulness of the material presented in this book.

It was essential to present meaningful and useful information to learners. The leadership principles presented must be logical and practical to all future leaders. Therefore, I would like to acknowledge the contributions of **Dr. Forest Kim, PhD, MBA. MHA. FACHE** for reviewing and advising on points in this book. As a clinical professor in the Department of Economics at the Hankamer School of Business, the Executive Director of the Robbins Institute for Health Policy and Leadership, and co-director of the Robbins Healthcare MBA program at Baylor University, Dr. Kim is uniquely qualified to review and edit this book. I would like to extend a personal thank you to Dr. Kim for his wise and thoughtful input. This book and its leadership concepts are better for his contributions.

As important as the leadership principles are in this book, the importance of interpreting and commenting on Holy Scripture is critical. Therefore, I would like to acknowledge the contributions of **Pastor Daniel Rowland**. Pastor Rowland serves as Student Pastor at Magnolia First Baptist Church in Magnolia, Texas. Pastor Rowland's commitment to examining God's word in detail and his principal commitment to teaching God's word accurately are highly commendable. His work with my target audience of Millennials and GenZ makes him uniquely qualified to comment not only on the book's accurate scriptural interpretation but also on the Millennial and GenZ groups. This book would not be possible without his reviews, comments, and contributions to accurately interpreting Bible verses. I cannot thank Pastor Rowland enough for his time, wisdom, honesty, and unwavering commitment to Biblical accuracy. Correct commentary of Biblical teachings truly creates a solid foundation for this book.

I wish to express my profound gratitude to my twin daughters Abby and Bailey, for their comments, advice, love, and support as I went through this writing process. Lastly, I would like to acknowledge God for guidance and wisdom. His words inspired, and His Holy Spirit guided the thoughts and process that brought this book to fruition.

Most gratefully,
Dr. Steven Purdon

Table of Contents

Preface

This book isn't your typical leadership guide. It's a practical training tool grounded in timeless wisdom from the Bible. Designed for busy leaders, it delivers short, actionable lessons that combine leadership principles with biblical insights.

If I were reading this book, I'd want to know the author's background. What makes them qualified to speak on leadership? Why should I invest my time in yet another leadership book?

This book is the result of over thirty years of experience in the healthcare industry, where I learned firsthand what works in leadership and what doesn't. Along the way, I discovered that effective leadership isn't just about making decisions; it's about pursuing a greater purpose.

As I reflected more deeply, I realized that the most powerful leadership principles are those that have stood the test of time. In a fast-changing world focused on self-interest, these enduring truths are more important than ever.

That's why this book introduces the concept of shepherd leadership, an approach rooted in biblical tradition yet adapted for today's challenges. It's a fresh, common-sense guide for those who want to lead with purpose and impact.

What is Shepherd leadership?

Shepherd leadership is a management approach that puts the needs of the team above those of the leader. It builds on the foundation of servant leadership but goes a step further introducing a fresh, forward-thinking leadership model that may require a cultural shift within your organization. This approach isn't just about being kind or supportive; it's about developing practical skills that enhance both how you manage and how your team performs.

At its core, shepherd leadership is rooted in empathy. It promotes a mindset where the leader consistently prioritizes the well-being and growth of others. Research has shown that leaders who place their teams and organizations ahead of personal ambition are often more effective and more successful We all want to be capable, impactful leaders, and this book is designed to help you get there by explaining the principles of shepherd leadership and offering the tools to apply them effectively.

Ask yourself:

- Are you dealing with disengaged or difficult employees?
- Is your organization facing high turnover?
- Do your leaders lack direction or clarity of vision?
- Are new or frontline managers struggling to lead effectively?

If any of these challenges sound familiar, this book offers real, actionable solutions.

Now, take a moment to imagine a shepherd tending to his flock. The image might seem quiet or even uneventful—a lone figure with a staff, keeping watch. But look closer. Over time, you'd see the shepherd is anything but passive. He is watchful, engaged, and deeply connected with each member of his flock. He knows their behaviors, their unique movements, their resting places in the grass, and even the sound of each one's bleat.

Remarkably, when the shepherd gives a command, the flock responds instantly. But if a stranger gives the same command, the flock pays no attention. Why? Because the shepherd has earned their trust through consistent presence, care, and familiarity.

Effective leaders operate the same way. They take time to understand their teams—not just as workers, but as individuals. And when that trust is built, leadership becomes far more powerful and productive.

Leader-follower paradigm.

What's more important: serving others or serving yourself?

At its core, leadership is about relationships. The dynamic between a leader and their team is no different from any other close human connection, it's built on trust, communication, and mutual respect. Yet many leaders forget that leadership isn't just about tasks and outcomes; it's about people.

Like any relationship, the one between a leader and their team can be either positive or negative. It might start off strong, then fade or fluctuate depending on how it's maintained. Relationships aren't always easy—they require patience, consistency, and effort. But when nurtured, they can become one of the most rewarding aspects of leadership.

Effective leadership doesn't happen in isolation. It's rooted in the strength of the relationship between the leader and those they serve. Building that connection takes time, intentional care, and a genuine commitment to putting others first.

Purpose of leadership

Leaders exist to inspire, provide direction, and guide their teams toward a common goal. But too often, leaders become distracted by day-to-day responsibilities or overly focused on personal achievements. When this happens, they can lose sight of how their actions affect those they lead.

It's easy for managers to fall into the trap of prioritizing tasks and metrics over people. But effective leadership requires the opposite mindset: leaders must remember that they are leaders first, and managers second. When ambition overrides awareness, teams suffer. In some cases, a leader's unchecked drive for personal success can do more harm than good.

So, why do we have leaders in the first place? The answer is simple: to move a group of people toward a shared goal. Leadership is essential to achieving results, but no leader can succeed alone. It takes a unified, motivated team. A leader's role is to cast a clear vision and communicate it effectively so the team can rally behind it.

That brings us to an important question: *What is the best way to lead a team to success?*

Over time, many leadership models have emerged such as transformational, transactional, situational, contingency, and trait theories, among others. Each offers valuable insights and provides useful frameworks for guiding leadership behavior and decision-making. These models help managers understand how to interact with their teams and how to align leadership style with context.

However, the workforce is changing. Millennials, Gen Z, and the emerging Gen Alpha employees are motivated by different values and expectations than previous generations.

They seek purpose, authenticity, connection, and flexibility in the workplace.

To lead them effectively, we need a new approach to leadership, one that goes beyond traditional theories and speaks to the needs of this new generation. That's where shepherd leadership comes in.

Shepherd Leadership for the next generation.

Shepherd leadership blends realism with optimism—two essential qualities that strongly appeal to the emerging generations of leaders. While Millennials are typically aspirational and idealistic, Generation Z brings a more grounded, pragmatic perspective. They plan for uncertainty and place high value on work-life balance, collaboration, empowerment, support, and flexibility. Generation Alpha—often called "upagers"—are displaying emotional maturity at earlier ages, suggesting a highly pragmatic and self-aware mindset in this rising generation.

Shepherd leadership speaks directly to these evolving values. It offers practical, actionable strategies for managing teams effectively, while also providing a hopeful and people-centered leadership framework that aligns with what younger generations seek in the workplace.

At the heart of this approach is emotional intelligence. This book is designed to help leaders strengthen their emotional awareness and empathetic reasoning—core traits that build trust, foster connection, and improve leadership effectiveness. In addition, it outlines a clear development plan for growing these competencies, helping the next generation of leaders lead with both empathy and effectiveness, in a way that resonates with their unique generational outlook.

Book layout

This book draws on thousands of years of biblical wisdom, paired with peer-reviewed, proven leadership strategies. The result is a powerful resource for leaders in any field—whether you're just starting your leadership journey or are a seasoned executive seeking to grow.

Each chapter is organized into four key sections to ensure clarity, depth, and practical application:

1. **The Verse**
2. **The Lesson**
3. **The Application**
4. **The Challenge**

These sections are clearly marked with subheadings for ease of reading. Together, they guide readers from timeless Scripture to real-world leadership practices.

The Verse

Every chapter begins with a Bible verse that highlights a relevant leadership principle. These verses offer insight and direction for anyone in a leadership role. Whether you're Christian, Jewish, agnostic, or simply curious about Scripture, many of these passages will feel familiar; or, at the very least, thought-provoking. Even if you don't consider yourself religious, you'll find that biblical wisdom often speaks to universal truths about character, responsibility, and influence.

The Lesson

Following each verse is a brief lesson that explores its meaning and context. Think of this as a mini-Bible study, one that builds a bridge from ancient wisdom to modern leadership. Each interpretation is rooted in sound biblical scholarship and proper hermeneutics. Understanding Scripture, or any meaningful writing, requires viewing it through the lens of the author's original intent. Whether it's ancient philosophy, sacred text, or modern poetry, context is key to drawing out its full meaning.

The Application

This is where theory meets practice. In this section, we translate the biblical lesson into actionable insights for today's workplace. Once a verse is understood in context, we ask: *What can this teach us about leading others?* These teachings provide practical, common-sense solutions to real leadership challenges. The goal here is too become not just a reader of Scripture, but a doer, someone who brings godly wisdom into their everyday decisions, interactions, and leadership style. These applications are designed to make you a more effective, empathetic, and purpose-driven leader.

The Challenge

This final section distills key takeaways from the application into a concise, bulleted list of actionable skills. These are the leadership habits and behaviors you can begin practicing right away. Think of it as your personal leadership growth checklist, a practical tool designed to help you apply what you've learned and take concrete steps toward becoming a more successful, servant-hearted leader.

Let's go learn something

Chapter 1
Shepherds Feed Their Lambs

The Verse

Ezekiel 34:2

"The word of the Lord came to me: ² "Son of man, prophesy against the shepherds of Israel; prophesy, and say to them, even to the shepherds, thus says the Lord God: Ah, shepherds of Israel who have been feeding yourselves! Should not shepherds feed the lamb?"

The Lesson

Ezekiel, whose name means *"God strengthens,"* was a true prophet of God living in Judea during the sixth century BC—a time marked by rebellion, hardship, and suffering. The leaders of Jerusalem had turned away from God, leading the people of Judah down a destructive path.

In the midst of this chaos, God chose Ezekiel to deliver messages revealing His will. In the verse referenced here, God rebukes the leaders of Judah, kings, priests, and false prophets, who were supposed to serve and protect the people. Instead, these "shepherds" were focused on their own interests. They neglected their responsibilities, and as a result, the people suffered and scattered.

1

God appoints leaders with a purpose: to care for, guide, and protect those under their influence. But the leaders of Judah failed in that mission. Rather than serving the flock, they served themselves. Their selfishness caused real harm.

The Application

A good shepherd always puts the needs of the flock before their own. That means practicing empathy, humility, and selflessness, qualities that aren't always easy or natural. For many leaders, these traits require ongoing self-awareness and intentional growth.

If you find it difficult to lead with empathy or humility, it's important to pause and reflect. Take an honest look at areas where personal weaknesses may be holding you back. When a leader is driven by arrogance or self-interest, it becomes nearly impossible to lead effectively or serve others well.

So how can you shift your mindset to truly prioritize your team? Start by asking yourself a few key questions to help reorient your leadership toward a *flock-first* approach:

- Am I making decisions that benefit the team or just myself?
- Do I listen more than I speak?
- Am I willing to admit when I'm wrong?
- How well do I understand the needs, strengths, and struggles of my team?

These questions are meant to guide you toward greater self-awareness and to help you cultivate a leadership style rooted in service, not self-interest. When shepherds lead with care, integrity, and selflessness, the flock thrives.

Understanding and Meeting the Needs of Your Lambs

As a shepherd leader, your primary responsibility is to know and care for your flock. One of the most effective ways to do this is by asking thoughtful, intentional questions. Here are six questions you can regularly use to check in with your team:

1. Do you have everything you need to perform your duties?
2. How can I help you today?
3. What barriers are you currently facing?
4. What type of work do you enjoy most?
5. How do you prefer to receive feedback?
6. What is your preferred communication style?

These questions help shift your focus to the needs of your lambs. Remember, those needs include both **tangible resources**, such as training materials, office supplies, and equipment, and **intangible resources** like work-life balance, clear policies, time off, competitive pay, and emotional support.

Take time to reflect: What do your lambs need? What obstacles are preventing them from thriving? Your ability to identify and address these issues will directly impact their morale and performance.

Listening and Talking

Strong leaders are strong listeners. To lead effectively, you must develop solid listening and communication skills. When you actively listen, you gain clarity on your team's true needs and can respond with care and intention. Listening is more than just hearing words—it's about understanding meaning and emotion.

Listen—Then Act

Listening is only half the equation. The most important step is follow-through. Once you've heard your team's concerns, you must take steps to address them. One of the most common and damaging leadership mistakes is listening without acting. When team members feel ignored, frustration and resentment quickly set in.

Your flock will always know when they're being overlooked. They may not say it outright, but they'll feel it, and their engagement will suffer. That's why action is essential. Address concerns when you can, and when you can't, explain why.

The Two Most Important Words: "Because" and "Why"

What should you do when a need cannot be met? Be honest and explain the reasoning. Two words will help you maintain trust and clarity: **because** and **why**.

Use them in your conversations:

- "I need you to do this **because**…"
- "We can't meet this request right now **because**…"
- "This is **why** we're moving in this direction…"

Using these two simple words accomplishes three critical things:

1. It builds stronger communication with your flock.
2. It shows your team that they matter and deserve an explanation.
3. It assures them they haven't been ignored or dismissed.

When used well, these words reduce confusion and prevent resentment from building. They show your team that you care enough to be transparent, an essential part of feeding your lambs.

Be Genuinely Interested

Get to know your lambs. Don't treat them as tasks to check off a list. Take a real interest in their individual needs, goals, and challenges. One-on-one meetings should never feel like a formality. If you're only meeting because it's required, your team will sense it.

Many organizations require regular check-ins, which is a good practice. But the impact of these meetings depends entirely on *how* they're conducted. A manager who says, "I've completed my quarterly one-on-one, so I'm done," is missing the point. Your lambs can tell when they're being treated like just another item on your to-do list.

The Challenge

Start building a *flock-first* mentality by putting these practical steps into action:

- **Strengthen your listening skills.** Make a conscious effort to truly hear your team—not just their words, but their concerns, motivations, and emotions.
- **Use the two most powerful words in leadership: "because" and "why."** These simple words provide clarity, show respect, and build trust through honest communication.
- **Identify barriers.** Regularly ask your team: *What obstacles are you facing?* Be proactive in removing or reducing those barriers.
- **Ask what your flock needs.** Create a spreadsheet or tracking document to record their needs. Review it regularly to ensure each item is being addressed and nothing falls through the cracks.

- **Treat your lambs as individuals, not checkboxes.** Every interaction should be personal and meaningful—not just something to cross off a list.

Chapter 2
Shepherds know their flock.

John 10:3-5

3 "To him the gatekeeper opens. The lamb hear his voice, and he calls his own lamb by name and leads them out. 4 When he has brought out all his own, he goes before them, and the lamb follow him, for they know his voice. 5 A stranger they will not follow, but they will flee from him, for they do not know the voice of strangers."

The Lesson

In this parable, Jesus teaches His disciples how a good shepherd cares for his lambs. A good shepherd calls each lamb by name and leads them because the lambs recognize and trust His voice. For those who follow Christ, Jesus is the Good Shepherd. We follow Him because we know and trust Him, and through studying Scripture, we learn to recognize His guidance. The lamb follows the shepherd because it knows and responds only to its trusted leader.

As the Good Shepherd, Jesus leads from the front, showing the way to safe, healthy, and nourishing pastures.

These verses emphasize that a good shepherd has a clear vision and will guide the flock to the right place. Jesus also points out that lambs will not follow strangers. To truly follow Him, we must know Him well, understanding Scripture is key to gaining wisdom and deepening our trust in God.

The Application

Go before them.

Experienced shepherds lead their flocks from the safety of the pen to pastures where they can graze and drink. The journey requires knowing the best routes to nourishment and water. Similarly, a leader must have a clear plan and understand the path to success. Good leaders ask themselves:

1. What is the goal for this month?
2. What obstacles might the flock face?
3. What resources does the flock need to reach the goal?
4. Have I communicated the plan clearly to my flock?

Knowing the answers helps a leader create a clear roadmap. It's essential that the flock understands the goal and their role in it. Like a shepherd leading from the front, a leader should be visible, present, and clear in communication. But don't get too far ahead, move at a pace the team can follow. Regular check-ins help ensure no one is left behind.

Know your flock.

Leadership is a two-way relationship. Just as Jesus calls each lamb by name, a good shepherd knows their flock deeply. How well do you know your team members? Their interests? Their families? Taking the time to build personal connections is crucial. Aristotle once said, *"You must eat a sack of salt with someone before you truly know them,"*

9

meaning relationships grow through shared time and experience.

Make it a priority to meet individually with your team regularly, whether for coffee or lunch, to show them they matter. Use this time not just to talk, but to listen deeply. Learn about their passions and challenges both inside and outside of work. Taking notes or creating simple profiles can help you remember and act on what you learn.

Your team members are more than just tasks to complete; they're individuals who thrive when leaders listen and empathize genuinely.

The Challenge

- Develop empathetic listening skills.
- Create a biography form for each team member.
- Schedule regular one-on-one time with each person.
- Set clear goals and communicate them to your team:
  - What is the goal for this month?
  - What obstacles might arise?
  - What resources are needed?
- Use one-on-one meetings to truly listen, not just hear, your team.

Chapter 3
Shepherds lead gently and effectively.

The Verse

Isaiah 40:11
"He will tend his flock like a shepherd; he will gather the lambs in his arms; he will carry them in his bosom and gently lead those that are with young."

The Lesson

This verse paints a powerful picture of God as the ultimate Shepherd, one who leads, protects, and nurtures His people with compassion and care. In Isaiah's time, sheep were essential to daily life. They provided wool, meat, milk, and were even used in sacred rituals. Because of their value; and vulnerability, they needed constant attention and a shepherd who could guide and protect them.

Throughout Scripture, God often compares us to sheep. Why? Because we behave in similar ways. We are easily influenced, emotionally driven, and not always aware of what's best for us. Like sheep, we require guidance and protection from someone wiser and stronger. God, as our Shepherd, leads us gently, especially when we are vulnerable, offering strength when we can't carry ourselves.

This verse reminds us of His tender care, especially for the weak and weary. It's a call for us, as leaders, to mirror that same spirit of gentleness and protection in our leadership roles.

The Application

Will I lead with force—or with compassion?

Domineering leaders may produce short-term results but often suffer from poor innovation, low morale, and reduced long-term success. In contrast, leaders who practice empathy and attentiveness foster environments where people thrive, emotionally, mentally, and professionally.

The Dangers of Shepherd Leadership

Like any leadership approach, shepherd leadership has its challenges. The most common is the risk of being overly compassionate. If a leader becomes too soft or overly accommodating, it can lead to complacency, a drop in accountability, and reduced productivity.

The good news? This can be avoided. The solution is balance:

- **Show empathy but maintain standards.**
- **Care deeply but keep your team accountable.**
- **Lead with heart but never lose sight of the goal.**

A good shepherd listens attentively and checks in regularly. They know when a lamb is struggling and step in to provide support. That support could be as simple as a listening ear, or as structured as offering external resources during times of crisis. Whether it's a personal loss, health issue, or financial stress, your lambs need to know you're there for them.

As the verse reminds us, the shepherd doesn't ignore the weak, he gathers them, carries them close, and leads gently.

Leadership isn't just about directing people; it's about understanding them. When one of your lambs is hurting, be ready to respond with patience, empathy, and a plan to help them return to strength.

Practical support may include:

- A conversation in a private setting
- A list of internal or external resources (HR, EAP, counseling services)
- Flexibility with schedules or workload during difficult times

Ultimately, helping your flock through hardship strengthens not just the individual but the entire flock.

The Challenge

- **Create space to connect with your flock.** Make time in your schedule to check in, not just when something goes wrong.
- **Prepare a resource list** to offer support when team members face personal struggles.
- **Hold your flock accountable.** Compassion does not mean lowering expectations, balance care with responsibility.

Chapter 4

Shepherds are held accountable.

The Verse

Ezekiel 34:7–10

7 "Therefore, you shepherds, hear the word of the LORD:
8 As surely as I live, declares the Sovereign LORD, because my flock lacks a shepherd and has been plundered and become food for all the wild animals, and because my shepherds did not search for my flock but cared for themselves rather than for my flock,
9 therefore, you shepherds, hear the word of the LORD:
10 This is what the Sovereign LORD says: I am against the shepherds and will hold them accountable for my flock. I will remove them from tending the flock so that the shepherds can no longer feed themselves. I will rescue my flock from their mouths, and it will no longer be food for them."

The Lesson

This passage comes from a time of deep crisis in Judah. Jerusalem had fallen to Babylon, many citizens were taken into exile, and the people were left feeling abandoned and vulnerable. In the middle of this chaos, God rebukes the leaders, referred to here as "shepherds", or their failure to care for His people.

These shepherds included kings, prophets, and religious leaders. Rather than guiding and protecting their people, they prioritized their own comfort and power. In verse 8, God highlights their selfishness: they ignored the flock's needs and allowed them to be plundered and devoured by "wild animals", a symbol of chaos, danger, and exploitation.

In verse 10, God issues a clear warning: He will hold these leaders accountable. He will remove them from their positions of influence and personally intervene to rescue His people. The message is sobering leadership is not just a title, but a divine responsibility. When leaders fail to serve and protect, there will be consequences.

The Application

Accountability Begins with You

Leadership comes with the serious responsibility of placing your team's needs ahead of your own. If you're leading only to maintain a title, earn a promotion, or please upper management, while neglecting the well-being of your people, you're missing the mark.

When leaders operate from self-interest, teams suffer. You'll see signs of this through:

- Low morale
- Poor job satisfaction

- High turnover
- Declining performance

Leaders who make decisions for personal gain often create toxic cultures that erode trust and productivity. Accountability means consistently evaluating your own motives and actions to ensure you're serving, not using, your people.

A Message to Senior Leadership

Many organizational problems trace back to ineffective leadership. For executives and upper management, it's essential to monitor not just performance metrics, but also the health of the culture underneath. Ask yourself:

1. What is the current **attrition rate**?
2. How is the team's **job satisfaction**?
3. Has **productivity** dropped off?

If the answers raise concern, start by examining the leader, not the team. Often, the issue lies in leadership failure.

What to Do with a Failing Shepherd

Not every struggling manager is beyond help. Sometimes failure stems from miscommunication, lack of training, or mismatched expectations. But regardless of the reason, leaders must be held accountable and given a path forward.

Steps to address leadership failure:

1. **Interview the leader** to understand their perspective.
2. **Talk to the team** the more lambs you speak to, the clearer the picture becomes.

3. **Reframe the failure** as a growth opportunity. Provide coaching or retraining if appropriate.
4. **Be willing to make a change.** If there's no improvement, it may be time to replace the leader for the good of the flock.

As Ezekiel reminds us, God values the safety and well-being of the flock above the comfort of the shepherd. The same must be true in your organization.

The Challenge

- Reflect honestly: **Why do you want to lead?** Is it about the title or the people?
- Check your priorities: **Are you leading for your own gain, or for your flock's success?**
- Evaluate your managers not just by numbers but by **the health and satisfaction of their teams**

Chapter 5
Shepherds are protectors

The Verse

Micah 5:4–6

*"And He shall stand and shepherd His
flock in the strength of the Lord, in the
majesty of the name of the Lord his God.
And they shall dwell secure, for now He
shall be great to the ends of the Earth."*

The Lesson

Micah, a prophet who lived between 750 and 687 BC,
ministered during the reigns of Jotham, Ahaz, and Hezekiah.
Coming from the rural town of Moresheth-Gath, far from the
hustle of urban centers, Micah often directed his prophecies
at the capital cities of Samaria and Jerusalem, calling out
their disobedience and corruption.

In this verse, Micah foresees the coming of a divine
Shepherd, Jesus Christ, who will lead His people with power,
authority, and humility. This Shepherd, empowered by the
majesty of God, will bring peace and safety to His flock. His
leadership will extend across the earth, establishing a
kingdom rooted in strength and security.

This passage reminds us that lasting peace and
strength do not come from human willpower alone. The
Shepherd's effectiveness comes from standing in the strength
of the Lord.

Likewise, leaders must recognize when they need support beyond their own abilities. As Philippians 4:13 states: "I can do all things through Christ who strengthens me." Not some things, but ALL things. But this requires humility, wisdom, and a willingness to rely on God's strength.

The Application

Micah 5:4–6 gives us two foundational principles for shepherd leadership:

1. **Shepherds must provide safety.**
   Just as a literal shepherd protects the flock from danger, good leaders create safe, supportive environments. When people feel secure, they're more likely to thrive, engage fully, and produce their best work.
2. **Shepherds must know when to rely on others.**
   Leadership is not a solo act. The most effective leaders know when to lean on the strengths of others—be it through delegation, collaboration, or simply asking for help.

Relying on Others

Even Jesus, in His humanity, demonstrated reliance on the Father. Likewise, we are called to lead with humility, trusting in God and the people He places around us.

As a leader, you may not have every answer, but your team might. Use the biographies you've developed (see Chapter One) to understand your lambs' unique strengths, then put those gifts to work.

Creating Task Forces

Instead of tackling every project on your own, build collaborative teams, or task forces, designed around the strengths of your flock.

Start by:

- Clarifying the goal
- Listing the steps and resources required
- Matching the right people with the right tasks

Doing so empowers your team, fosters collaboration, and increases buy-in.

! **Caution:** Task forces can increase individual workloads.

Be mindful of burnout and overcommitment. Protect your flock by monitoring their capacity and providing support when needed.

Bringing Peace and Safety to the Flock

True shepherd leaders understand and anticipate threats. Just like a shepherd watching for wolves, you must identify hazards before they harm your flock.

Three Areas of Potential Danger:

1. **Internal (workplace)** – Overwork, harassment, insufficient training, ergonomic hazards, etc.
2. **External (outside of work)** – Family conflict, financial stress, health issues
3. **Personal (within the employee)** – Mental health struggles, fatigue, substance abuse

Watch for red flags:

- Sudden dips in productivity
- Missed deadlines or poor performance
- Absenteeism or withdrawal
- Changes in behavior or attitude

These may indicate a lamb is in distress. Don't ignore the signs. Gently check in and offer support.

Watch Productivity Levels

Productivity is a pulse check on the health of your team. If you're noticing declines, ask yourself:

- Is fear stifling communication?
- Are my people overwhelmed?
- Do they feel valued?

Fear often shuts down open dialogue. Combat this by building trust through **empathetic listening**. Sit down one-on-one, listen without judgment, and offer reassurance and support.

The Power of Recognition

Recognition goes beyond pay, it acknowledges effort and reinforces value.

When people feel seen, they feel safe.

Create a recognition strategy tailored to your team's needs. Ideas include:

- Public shout-outs during meetings
- Handwritten thank-you notes
- Gift cards or small rewards

- Offering extra time off
- Celebrating milestones or birthdays

The most important part? Make it personal. Know what motivates each lamb.

Dealing with Stress

Stress is a natural part of any job, but if left unchecked, it can grow into fear and burnout. Leaders must be vigilant.

Common stressors include:

- Unrealistic deadlines
- Role ambiguity
- Personal issues at home
- Lack of work-life balance

Be proactive. Don't wait for a crisis. Ask questions, observe, and intervene early.

Strategies to Reduce Fear

Micah teaches us that when a shepherd stands strong, the flock feels secure.

Here's how to reduce fear in your team:

- **Practice empathy.** Understand the "why" behind stress.
- **Offer practical solutions.** Don't just listen; act.
- **Be present.** Consistent engagement creates safety.
- **Balance workloads.** If someone's newly promoted, consider easing their burden or helping with time management.

- **Encourage self-care.** Suggest hobbies, breaks, or resources like counseling or financial advising when needed.

Let your team know they are not alone. Solutions exist and you are there to help find them.

The Challenge

- **Plan team-building events** to foster connection and lower isolation.
- **Identify internal, external, and personal risks** that may impact your flock.
- **Develop a recognition strategy** that fits your culture and team.
- **Learn the signs of stress** and burnout before they become crises.
- **Practice active listening** to uncover the root causes and act.

When you walk beside your flock, recognizing their strengths, easing their burdens, and protecting their well-being, you create a culture of safety, trust, and resilience. That's what true shepherd leadership looks like.

Chapter 6
Shepherds closely supervise their flocks.

The Verse

1 Peter 5:2–3

"Shepherd the flock of God that is among you, exercising oversight, not under compulsion, but willingly, as God would have you; not for shameful gain, but eagerly; not domineering over those in your charge, but being examples to the flock."

The Lesson

Peter wrote this letter to leaders in the early church; those guiding communities in places like Pontus, Galatia, Cappadocia, Asia, and Bithynia. His goal was to offer encouragement and guidance as the Gospel spread across the region. In this passage, Peter shares important insight on how leaders should care for those entrusted to them.

He begins by emphasizing the heart behind leadership. Leaders should not serve out of obligation or external pressure, but out of a genuine desire to care for others. Leadership, in Peter's view, is not a burden to carry, but a calling to embrace.

Next, he warns against selfish motivation, especially the pursuit of personal gain. The role of a shepherd isn't about status, power, or money; it's about the well-being of the flock.

Finally, Peter reminds leaders not to be domineering. The shepherd doesn't lead with force or fear, but by example. The strength of a true leader is found not in control, but in influence through character.

The Application

Peter's message is timeless. Though he wrote to early church leaders, the advice is just as relevant for anyone in a leadership role today. His words give us a simple and powerful framework for shepherd leadership, highlighting **what to avoid** and **what to embrace**.

The Don'ts

Let's start with Peter's warnings; his **"don'ts"** for leaders.

1. **Don't lead out of obligation.**
   If your leadership is motivated only by your paycheck, your job title, or pressure from others, you're missing the point. Leading with a reluctant heart lead to burnout, resentment, and poor performance. Ask yourself:

   Am I leading because I want to or because I feel like I have to? If it's the latter, your team will eventually feel your lack of commitment.

2. **Don't lead for selfish gain.**
   If your primary motivation is money, recognition, or the prestige of being "in charge," your leadership will

lack depth. These rewards may come, but they should never be your "why." If your focus is on yourself, your flock will be neglected.

3. **Don't domineer.**
   Controlling leaders erode trust. When you dominate rather than guide, you create fear instead of respect. True shepherds lead with gentleness, clarity, and compassion, earning loyalty through example, not force.

The Do's

Now let's focus on Peter's **"do's."**

1. **Lead willingly.**
   Approach leadership as a privilege, not a duty. When you lead with eagerness and joy, your team will feel it. That attitude becomes contagious.
2. **Lead with the right intent.**
   Take a moment for some honest reflection:
   o *Why do I want to be in management?*
   o *Why do I want to be a leader?*
      Think about your answers. Are they centered on service—or status? If you answered, "to be the boss," it might be time to reassess your approach and realign with a heart of service.
3. **Lead by example.**
   This is Peter's core message. If you want your team to work hard, be honest, collaborate, and stay focused—then you must embody those traits first. Your flock is always watching. Let them see the leader you want them to become.

The Challenge

Ready to step into shepherd leadership? Start with these four simple actions:

- **Perform a self-examination** – Ask yourself: *Why do I really want to be a leader?*
- **Lead by example** – Don't lead with control, lead with character.
- **List the attributes of a good lamb** – Think about what makes a great team member.
- **Live those attributes out** – Model them in your daily actions for all to see.

Final Thought

Peter reminds us that leadership isn't about power or perks—it's about purpose. A shepherd leads not for status, but for service. When your heart is in the right place and your actions reflect your values, you'll lead a flock that trusts you, follows you, and grows under your care.

Chapter 7
Shepherds' standby their flock.

The Verse

Zechariah 11:17

*"Woe to my worthless shepherd, who
deserts the flock! May the sword strike his
arm and his right eye! Let his arm be
wholly withered, his right eye utterly
blinded!"*

The Lesson

In Zechariah 11, we see a stark warning about the
consequences of poor leadership. The imagery is strong,
harsh, even but it serves a purpose. The shepherd who
neglects or abandons the flock is not only labeled "worthless"
but is also cursed with a withered arm and a blinded eye.
While these descriptions may be metaphorical, they
emphasize God's intense disapproval of irresponsible
leadership.

This chapter was written during a time of political
instability, reflecting a deeper spiritual truth: God expects
leaders, whether kings, priests, prophets, or modern-day
managers, to care for those entrusted to them. When they
don't, there are consequences. The symbolism of a withered
arm (a loss of strength) and a blinded eye (a loss of vision)
reflects what happens when a leader fails: they lose the very
qualities that made them fit to lead.

Romans 13:1 tells us that all authority comes from God, and those in positions of leadership are placed there by Him. With that authority comes responsibility, and with responsibility comes accountability.

The Application

Until now, we've focused on the benefits of being a good shepherd. But Zechariah reminds us that **neglect has consequences**. Leadership isn't just about the perks, it's about stewardship. And when a leader fails to serve their people, both the flock and the leader suffer.

There is a growing issue in the workplace: employees are expressing concerns more frequently and showing signs of lower productivity. What was the common thread? **Managers were listening but not following through.** Team members left meetings feeling unheard, unsupported, and ultimately neglected.

It's easy for leaders to "check the box" by holding team meetings or conducting performance reviews. But if those meetings end with no meaningful follow-up, the result is the same as abandonment. It's not enough to hear—**you must act**.

We see this all too often in performance improvement plans. A quarterly one-on-one is scheduled, notes are taken, and then… nothing happens. The leader may believe they've done their job by meeting, but if concerns are never addressed, morale suffers, and trust erodes.

Shepherd leadership flips this model. A shepherd doesn't just listen, they respond. They understand that their flock consists of individuals with real needs and challenges. If you genuinely care, you'll persist until the issue is resolved. That kind of engagement is what creates thriving teams and successful organizations.

A Message for Upper Management

If you're in senior leadership, this next part is for you.

Shepherd leadership takes time, and your frontline managers are your shepherds, and they need **space** to learn and grow into their role. If you pile on responsibilities without giving them room to connect with their teams, don't be surprised when engagement drops and turnover rises.

You can't expect your shepherds to lead well if they're drowning in administrative tasks or pulled in ten directions. Give them protected time to meet with their teams. Encourage monthly one-on-ones, and most importantly, **follow up with your shepherds** just as you ask them to follow up with their teams.

Everything we've discussed about tending the flock applies to **your leadership team** as well. Your managers are your flock. They need guidance, encouragement, and resources just like everyone else.

Be a **shepherd of shepherds**.

Help them grow into the leaders your organization needs. Equip them. Empower them. Support them. When you invest in your leaders, they'll invest in theirs and the impact will ripple throughout your entire organization.

- **Follow through after listening.** Don't stop at hearing; take meaningful action.
- **Be a consistent and present leader.** Shepherds don't visit the flock once and disappear.
- **Make time for one-on-ones.** Prioritize face-to-face connections each month.
- **Support your shepherds.** Give managers what they need to care for their teams effectively.
- **Lead with conviction.** Don't be the "worthless shepherd" who deserts their flock.

The Challenge

- Plan to meet with your lambs individually on a regular basis.
- Create a meeting notebook to record concerns expressed by the lamb.
- Follow up on any concerns your lambs may express.
- Reevaluate the number of duties your managers have.
- Upper leaders must ensure their shepherds are meeting with their lambs and have the time to do it.

Final Thought

Zechariah's message may sound intense, but it's rooted in love. God deeply values the people in our care and expects leaders to do the same. A neglected flock will scatter. A supported flock will thrive. Your leadership matters. Don't desert your people. Shepherd them with care, conviction, and purpose.

Chapter 8
Shepherds show love and grace.

The Verse

Jeremiah 23:3

"Then I will gather the remnant of my flock out of all the countries where I have driven them, and I will bring them back to their fold, and they shall be fruitful and multiply."

The Lesson

In the early 600s BC, Jeremiah witnessed Judah's decline as the people turned away from God. Israel had already fallen to Assyria, and now Babylon was at Jerusalem's gates. Because of their disobedience, God allowed His people to be conquered and scattered.

But even in judgment, there's hope. In this verse, God promises to gather the **remnant**, those who remained faithful, and bring them back to safety. Once restored, they would flourish again.

This is a powerful message of **grace**. Even when we stray from God, He offers a way back. No matter how many steps you've taken away from God, it only takes one step to return. When His people returned to Him, He restored them to their rightful place and they became fruitful.

Later in Jeremiah, we read, *"Pray that the LORD your God may tell us the way we should walk and the thing we should do"* (Jer. 42:3). Knowing what God expects is the first step toward restoration and productivity. When we turn from sin and follow Him, forgiveness leads to flourishing.

The Application

1. Shepherds Restore the Flock

A good shepherd plays an active role in restoring the flock. God didn't wait for His people to return on their own; He *gathered* them. That's the model for us as leaders: we don't just wait; we lead the way.

Jeremiah says God brought them "back to their fold"; their proper place. A restored flock thrives when it's where it's supposed to be. **Where does your team belong?** As a leader, it's your job to clearly communicate goals, clarify roles, and guide your team to a place of unity and productivity.

📌 *Lead with clarity—ensure everyone understands the vision, their roles, and how their efforts contribute to the whole.*

2. Watch for the Wayward Lamb

Not everyone will stay on course. Sometimes team members, just like sheep, stray. How we respond can make or break trust within the group.

A strong leader knows how to **balance accountability with grace**. There are certainly times when discipline is necessary. But there are also moments when a gentle response does more to restore than punish.

🖈 *Ask yourself: Do I have a clear strategy for handling mistakes? Does it include empathy and second chances when appropriate?*

3. Understand Before You Act

To handle wayward team members well, start with **empathy**. And the first step to empathy is **listening**.

Meet privately. Ask thoughtful, non-accusatory questions. Listen more than you speak. Try to get to the *root* of the issue before deciding how to respond. Then, clearly explain your expectations going forward.

🖈 *People are more likely to accept correction when they know they've been heard.*

4. Offer Encouragement

Correction should always be followed by **encouragement**. It shows grace and reinforces that the person is still valued.

In difficult moments, encouragement carries even more weight. A few words of support can rebuild confidence and remind someone that you believe in them, even when mistakes happen.

🖈 *Encouragement in tough times is leadership at its finest.*

The Challenge

As a shepherd-leader, ask yourself:

- Have I clearly communicated our **vision and goals**?
- Does every team member know their **responsibilities**, including mine?
- Do I know how to **recognize and restore** a struggling team member?
- Am I listening *fully* before reacting?
- Do I know when to show **grace**, and when to act?
- Have I developed a plan for offering **encouragement**, especially after correction?

Make it a priority this week to:

- Clarify roles and responsibilities.
- Create a checklist for handling wayward team members with empathy and discipline.
- List ways to encourage your team—both in good times and tough ones.

Final Thought

Just as God gathered His people and restored them, leaders today are called to **restore**, **guide**, and **nurture** their teams. When you create a culture of clarity, compassion, and accountability, your team will not only return to the fold; but will also be **fruitful and multiply**.

Chapter 9
Shepherds don't neglect their sheep.

The Verse

> ### Jeremiah 23:1-2
> *"Woe to the shepherds who destroy and scatter the sheep of my pasture!" declares the Lord.*
> *2 "Therefore, this is what the Lord, the God of Israel, says to the shepherds who tend my people: 'Because you have scattered my flock and driven them away and have not bestowed care on them, I will bestow punishment on you for the evil you have done,' declares the Lord."*

The Lesson

Jeremiah prophesied in Jerusalem during the early to mid-600s BC. He was a messenger of both warning and hope to the people of Judah. Despite his urgent warnings, the people ignored him, and he was ultimately proven right. In 586 BC, Jerusalem was destroyed by the Babylonians, and its people were taken into exile.

In these verses, God delivers a direct warning to the "shepherds" of Judah, its leaders: kings, priests, and false prophets. These leaders had failed in their responsibilities. Instead of guiding the people in righteousness, they allowed idol worship, tolerated foreign altars to false gods, and neglected their duty to teach and uphold God's covenant. As a result, the flock (God's people) became scattered, confused, and spiritually lost.

God's warning is clear: because these shepherds neglected their flock, He would now deal with them personally. This powerful message emphasizes how seriously God takes leadership and the consequences of neglecting those entrusted to our care.

The Application

When a flock is left unattended, it becomes vulnerable. Without direction, people lose focus, become divided, and fail to achieve the mission. A shepherd's primary role is to provide guidance, unity, and protection. The failure to lead results in chaos and ultimately, in failure.

A Safe Environment Leads to Growth

People thrive when they feel safe, free from fear, hostility, or neglect. Verse 4 of this chapter reveals God's promise to care for and protect His flock after removing the corrupt leaders. Good shepherds reflect this by ensuring their teams feel secure.

Here are a few reflection questions for leaders:

- Does your team know you have their backs in difficult situations?
- Are they working in an environment free of harassment or discrimination?
- Are you vigilant about physical and emotional safety in the workplace?

A protected and supported team is more productive, less anxious, and better equipped to succeed.

How to Build Trust

Trust doesn't happen instantly; it takes time and intentional effort. While we might give people the benefit of the doubt, genuine trust is earned through consistent behavior. As a shepherd, it's your responsibility to take the first step.

Effective trust-building requires:

1. **Honesty** – Be transparent and tell the truth, even when it's difficult.
2. **Integrity** – Always do the right thing, not just when it's convenient.
3. **Humility** – Admit when you're wrong and be open to correction.
4. **Sacrifice** – Put the needs of your team ahead of your own when necessary.

Building trust means being present. Spend time with your team, get to know what motivates them, and recognize their individual strengths. Leaders who remain distant risk losing perspective and can easily begin to treat people as cogs in a machine rather than valued individuals.

Intent Isn't Enough

You may have good intentions, but if your actions don't reflect them, your team won't feel supported. Policies, behaviors, and communication all send a message. Take time to examine how your intentions are perceived. Do your actions align with your values? Are your policies fair and clearly understood?

The Challenge

- Make sure your team knows you're in their corner.

- Review your policies to ensure they reflect your core values.
- Provide regular, constructive feedback.
- Align your actions with your intentions.
- Spend time with your team to build authentic, lasting trust.

Chapter 10
Shepherds will lead their flocks forward.

The Verses

Zechariah 13:7
"Awake, O sword, against my shepherd,
against the man who stands next to me,"
declares the Lord of hosts.
"Strike the shepherd, and the sheep will be
scattered;
I will turn my hand against the little
ones."

Zechariah 10:2 (b)
"...Therefore the people wander like
sheep;
they are afflicted for lack of a shepherd."

Matthew 9:36
"When He saw the crowds, He had
compassion on them,
because they were harassed and
helpless, like sheep without a shepherd."

The Lesson

In this chapter, we're given three powerful verses that emphasize one essential truth: *a flock without a shepherd is vulnerable, disoriented, and at risk of being lost or destroyed*

Historical Context of Zechariah

Zechariah was both a priest and prophet during the time of Israel's return from exile in Babylon (circa 520–518 BC). Though King Cyrus of Persia allowed the Jews to return to Judea around 538 BC, the restoration process was slow and disheartening. The Temple had only a foundation laid after decades of attempts, and the people felt abandoned by God. Yet through Zechariah, God reminded them that even *small beginnings* mattered to Him (Zechariah 4:10). God rejoiced when His people took even small steps forward.

Zechariah 13:7 – A Struck Shepherd and Scattered Sheep

This verse prophetically refers to Jesus Christ, the Shepherd, who would be struck (crucified), leading His followers to scatter. Jesus Himself quoted this verse in Matthew 26:31 just before His arrest. The "sword" represents God's judgment, and Jesus willingly became the Lamb slain for the sins of the world.

Despite the scattering, God promises in the final line of the verse that He will still care for the "little ones"—those faithful to Him. The key takeaway is that even when chaos ensues, *God is in control,* and His protection remains over the faithful. A good shepherd doesn't just guide; he protects, even through hardship.

Zechariah 10:2b – Wandering Without a Shepherd

Here, we see the result of spiritual and political leadership failure. No Davidic king had returned, and God had removed previous leaders due to corruption. As a result, the people wandered aimlessly, feeling abandoned and lost. This verse reinforces the need for godly leadership, a shepherd who can guide, unify, and care for the flock.

Matthew 9:36 – Jesus' Compassion for the Shepherd
less

Jesus, seeing the spiritual state of the crowds, had
compassion. He viewed them as "harassed and helpless,"
much like sheep without a shepherd. This wasn't just about
leadership; it was about *care.* The people were vulnerable
because no one was actively shepherding them with truth and
love.

The Application

When we combine the message from all three verses,
a consistent truth emerges: *Without strong, engaged
leadership, people scatter.* Scattered teams are unproductive,
discouraged, and often overwhelmed. Today, this principle is
just as true in the workplace as it was in biblical times.

Leaders must stay involved and actively guide their
teams. In a modern context, especially with more remote
work and dispersed teams, this role is more critical than ever.

And just like God celebrated even the smallest steps
toward rebuilding the Temple, leaders today should
encourage and guide progress, even when it's incremental.

Two Key Concepts to Hold Your Team Together

1. Aligning Your Team as One Unit

Alignment means everyone is focused on the same goals and
moving in the same direction. When your team is aligned:

- Efforts are unified.
- Communication improves.
- Morale and performance increase.

How to align your team:

- Set meaningful goals.
- Clarify team priorities.
- Define responsibilities and expectations.
- Regularly remind the team of key objectives.
- Track progress and provide feedback.
- Hold team members accountable.
- Communicate clearly, consistently, and often.

🏹 *William A. Schiemann defines alignment as "the extent to which employees are similarly connected to, or have a consistent line of sight to, the vision and direction of the organization and its customers."* (Performance Management, p. 47)

2. Aligning Teams with the Organization

Once your team is unified, it's important to ensure they are also aligned with the organization's broader goals. When all teams work together toward shared objectives, the organization functions with greater harmony and efficiency.

For upper-level leaders:

- Use the same alignment strategies—set clear goals, track progress, communicate often.
- Ensure departments are working toward shared objectives.
- Understand and respond to customer needs.
- Stay aware of how your brand is perceived—by customers *and* competitors.

The Challenge

Act with these practical steps:

Use SMART Goals
(Specific, Measurable, Achievable, Relevant, Time-Bound)

- Be clear and realistic about what you're aiming for.
- Set reminders to track progress.
- Communicate expectations clearly and frequently.

Reinforce team and organizational goals regularly

- Don't assume your team remembers the goals repetition creates clarity.

Engage with customers and employees often

- Seek feedback from both.
- Stay connected to their needs and concerns.

Build trust and unity daily

- Don't wait for problems to arise.
- Be proactive in shepherding your flock.

Chapter 11
Shepherds are there for their flocks.

The Verse

Isaiah 53:6
"All we like sheep have gone astray;
we have turned—every one—to his own
way;
and the Lord has laid on him
the iniquity of us all."

The Lesson

We have all sinned and fallen short of the glory of God. As Isaiah states, "All we like sheep have gone astray," meaning that every person has turned away from God to follow their own path. This speaks to the reality of *original sin*—that our nature is to drift from God's will and do what seems right in our own eyes.

Isaiah reinforces this truth again in chapter 64:6: **"All of us have become like one who is unclean, and all our righteous deeds are like a filthy garment."**

The Apostle Paul echoes this theme in his letter to the Romans:

- **Romans 1:20:** *"All are guilty and without excuse."*
- **Romans 3:10:** *"There is none righteous, not even one."*

The message is clear: **sin is universal**, and **every person is in need of a Savior**.

But Isaiah 53:6 doesn't leave us hopeless. The second half brings redemption:
"And the Lord has laid on Him the iniquity of us all."
This refers to Jesus Christ, the Good Shepherd, who willingly took upon Himself the full weight of our sin through His sacrifice on the cross. The penalty for sin is death, and Jesus paid that price—on our behalf—so we could be forgiven and restored to right relationship with God.

The Application

So, what does this have to do with leadership?

God often uses the image of sheep to describe people because sheep, by nature, tend to wander without guidance. This verse reminds us that people, too, need a shepherd to keep them focused and protected.

As a leader, *you are the shepherd* for your team. It's your responsibility to:

- Be present.
- Provide direction.
- Offer care and support.
- Keep the flock unified and on track so they won't go astray.

If you're a leader who only shows up when there's a problem or hides behind a closed office door your team will begin to drift, lose focus, and feel disconnected. Sheep without a shepherd are left vulnerable, and so are employees without engaged leadership.

Executive Ground Rounds

One of the best ways to stay connected with your team is through *executive ground rounds*. This concept refers to leaders regularly walking through their departments, job sites, or offices to engage directly with staff.

But ground rounds aren't just for executives, **leaders at every level** should make time to visit and check in with their teams. Greet people, ask how their day is going, listen to concerns, and be approachable. Speak to everyone from frontline workers to support staff. When you're visible and accessible, barriers come down, trust increases, and people feel valued.

Why is this important?

Because a flock that sees its shepherd often is less likely to wander. You'll also gain firsthand insight into the needs and morale of your organization, allowing you to make smarter, more informed decisions.

Can't walk the halls?

Maybe your team is spread across multiple counties, or you're managing a construction site. That's okay, **make time to visit anyway.** Show up in person. Even a small effort to be physically present speaks volumes and strengthens relationships.

The Value of Personal Touches

In today's fast-paced digital world, personal connection is becoming rare but it's more important than ever. Texts and video calls are convenient, but they often lack the warmth and connection of a face-to-face interaction.

Ask yourself:

When was the last time you sat down one-on-one with a team member?

If it's been a while, that's your sign; it's time to reconnect.

Personal gestures go a long way. A handwritten note. A quick, face-to-face check-in. A meaningful word of encouragement. These seemingly small actions have lasting impact and let your team know they are seen, valued, and not just another cog in the wheel.

The Challenge

- **Don't just take time; *make* time** for your people.
- **Write a handwritten note** to show appreciation.
- **Establish a regular schedule for executive ground rounds.**
- **Prioritize face-to-face interactions** with your team.

The more present and intentional you are as a shepherd, the less likely your flock will stray and the stronger and more unified your team will become.

Chapter 12
Shepherds must understand their gifts.

The Verse

Ephesians 4:11–14

*"And he gave the apostles, the prophets,
the evangelists, the shepherds and
teachers,
to equip the saints for the work of ministry,
for building up the body of Christ,
until we all attain to the unity of the faith
and of the knowledge of the Son of God,
to mature manhood, to the measure of the
stature of the fullness of Christ,
so that we may no longer be children,
tossed to and fro by the waves
and carried about by every wind of
doctrine, by human cunning, by craftiness
in deceitful schemes."*

The Lesson

The Apostle Paul writes to the believers in Ephesus, reminding them that God has gifted each of us for a purpose. Some are called to be apostles, prophets, evangelists, shepherds, or teachers but all gifts are given for the same reason: **to build up the body of Christ**.

These roles are not given for self-glory but to serve the church, to equip others for ministry, and to help bring the church to spiritual maturity. When we use our gifts well, Paul says we grow in unity, knowledge, and character ultimately becoming more like Christ. This process of growing in faith and obedience is known as *sanctification*. It's a lifelong journey of becoming more like Christ.

Paul also warns that without this maturity; we are easily deceived, tossed around by every new idea or false teaching. But when we live out our calling, grounded in truth and obedience, we are no longer spiritual children but mature believers, discerning and stable.

The takeaway is clear:
Discover your God-given gifts and use them to serve others. In doing so, you strengthen the church, glorify Christ, and grow into the leader God has called you to be.

The Application

Step 1: Know Your Strengths

Each of us has unique talents and strengths that can be used to serve our teams and organizations. But to use them effectively, we must first **recognize what they are**.

Here are some reflective questions to help identify your strengths:

- What am I naturally good at?
- What work energizes and excites me?
- What tasks do I enjoy?
- What traits have others consistently praised in me?

Once you identify your strengths, ask:
How can I use these gifts to better serve my team (or flock)?
Here are a few practical examples:

- Are you a great teacher? Consider offering monthly training sessions.
- Skilled in setting goals? Align your team to overcome obstacles strategically.
- Good at diplomacy? Step into situations of conflict and help mediate resolutions.

Step 2: Acknowledge Your Weaknesses

Knowing your weaknesses is just as valuable as knowing your strengths. Self-awareness leads to growth.

Ask yourself:

- What tasks drain me?
- What skills do I consistently struggle with?
- What have others given me constructive feedback about?

After identifying weaknesses, prioritize them by how much they impact your ability to lead. Then, make a plan to improve.

Examples:

1. **Public Speaking**
   Uncomfortable speaking in front of groups? Start small practice with family or close colleagues. The more you do it, the more confident you'll become.
2. **Communication**
   If you struggle with communication, study what makes for effective communication: clarity, listening, tone, and timing. Then apply it intentionally.
3. **Organization**
   o Make daily task lists.
   o Prioritize them by importance and urgency.
   o Use digital tools or calendars to stay on top of responsibilities.

The formula is simple:

1. Identify the weakness.
2. Practice improving it.

It doesn't need to be complicated; just consistent.

Becoming a Better Shepherd

Leadership requires introspection. The more you know about yourself—your abilities, your gaps, your passions—the more effective you'll be in leading others.

Use your strengths to bless your flock. Work on your weaknesses to better serve them. As you grow, your team will grow. And along the way, you'll gain greater wisdom, maturity, and impact.

The Challenge

- **List your strengths** and create activities that utilize them to strengthen your team.
- **List your weaknesses** and begin a deliberate plan to improve them.
- **Reflect regularly**, and track how your growth as a leader is helping your flock thrive.

Remember, a good shepherd knows both his gifts and his gaps—and is committed to growth for the sake of the flock he serves.

Final thoughts.

Shepherd Leadership: A Higher Calling

Being a good leader is more than just being a boss; it's a selfless responsibility. True leadership involves caring for others while working together to achieve shared goals.

Shepherd leadership is a cultural shift that builds upon servant leadership. Shepherd leaders consistently act in their team's best interests, understanding that a thriving flock leads to organizational success. This fosters higher job satisfaction, reduces turnover, and lowers operational costs and financial performance.

Though the term may feel new, shepherd leadership is not a modern invention. Its principles are rooted in timeless wisdom. This book guides leaders at every level toward lasting success, requiring a mindset shift or structural changes within the organization. The long-term reward is a profitable and rewarding workplace for everyone involved.

Great leaders inspire others, provide clear direction, and reach goals with their teams, not above them. Leadership depends on relationships, which take time, trust, and intentional effort.

As you apply the lessons in this book, you'll see real trust forming between you and your flock. May you grow together, serve each other well, and build an organization that others want to be part of for all the right reasons.

Prayers for your flock.

As a Shepherd leader, dedicating prayer time for your team is a good idea. The following prayers are suggestions only. Of course, you do not have to use these, but hopefully, this section will serve as a reminder to pray daily for your flock, those lambs that may be struggling with life issues, and your organization.

Prayer for your flock.

Heavenly Father, I lift my team up to you today. May you guide their decisions and bless the work of their hands. I ask for their protection as they travel to and from work and that you keep them safe while at work. In Jesus' name. Amen.

For the struggling lamb.

Almighty God, you are Jehovah Rapha, the God who heals, and Jehovah Jireh, the God who provides. I humbly ask that you provide for the needs of NAME OF LAMB. Please be there for HIM/HER and provide comfort and grant peace to HIM/HER at this time. Draw close to, NAME OF LAMB, and let HIM/HER know that HE/SHE can call upon you to give strength and guidance in this challenging time. In Jesus' name. Amen.

For your organization.

Heavenly Father, I ask that you give direction to all the leaders in our organization and give them discernment to make the right decisions that are best for the company and its people. In Jesus' name. Amen.

For me, their shepherd.

Lord, please give me the strength to make difficult decisions. Please grant me discernment to make the right calls and help me lead humbly, as You will require me to do. Lead me in understanding and give me wisdom. In Jesus' name. Amen

About the Author

Dr. Steven Purdon brings over 25 years of clinical and leadership experience across a wide range of healthcare settings; from private practices to his role as Hospital Director aboard the *Global Mercy*, a floating charity hospital with complex operational demands.

He teaches graduate-level healthcare leadership at top U.S. universities and is the author of *Healing Leadership, Unlocking the Power of Shepherd Leadership in Healthcare.*

Dr. Purdon blends clinical expertise, practical leadership insight, and a servant's heart to help leaders create people-centered, purpose-driven impact in healthcare.

He is also a devoted Christ follower and a proud father.